Cory Contini

Globalization and Sovereignty through Conflict

A precise breakdown of how society adapts

GRIN Verlag

Bibliografische Information der Deutschen Nationalbibliothek:

Die Deutsche Bibliothek verzeichnet diese Publikation in der Deutschen National-
bibliografie; detaillierte bibliografische Daten sind im Internet über http://dnb.d-
nb.de/ abrufbar.

Imprint:

Copyright © 2009 GRIN Verlag GmbH
Druck und Bindung: Books on Demand GmbH, Norderstedt Germany
ISBN: 978-3-656-46331-3

This book at GRIN:

http://www.grin.com/en/e-book/230473/globalization-and-sovereignty-through-
conflict

GRIN - Your knowledge has value

Der GRIN Verlag publiziert seit 1998 wissenschaftliche Arbeiten von Studenten, Hochschullehrern und anderen Akademikern als eBook und gedrucktes Buch. Die Verlagswebsite www.grin.com ist die ideale Plattform zur Veröffentlichung von Hausarbeiten, Abschlussarbeiten, wissenschaftlichen Aufsätzen, Dissertationen und Fachbüchern.

Visit us on the internet:

http://www.grin.com/

http://www.facebook.com/grincom

http://www.twitter.com/grin_com

Globalisation and Sovereignty through Conflict

by Cory Contini

May 2010

Globalisation has brought about fundamental change. Advancements in technology have made the global markets more accessible than ever before making trade and investing abroad much more efficient. It has become so easy to reach the global population that it would be detrimental for any entity not to expand its horizons; however, the question on whether or not an entity should go global raises conflict right from the start.

Trading, in general, makes it more likely for conflict between countries due to natural trade relations; however, globalisation mitigates these problems. Conflict is innately involved in trading and trying to maximize one's own position but globalisation has brought information and resources closer to the trader allowing for faster and more informed decision making. So although conflicts may arise, globalisation helps to extinguish the conflict faster.

NAFTA is a trilateral agreement between the U.S., Canada, and Mexico which allows for free trade within North America. Although there is a section in NAFTA that specifically deals with conflicts between member countries, in general, the agreement makes it easier to do trade or invest by globalising the continent. That's not to say conflict doesn't arise because it quite frequently does; it just happens less often because the ground rules are well established.

Currently, the basic conflict in globalisation is based on dependency. From this perspective, developing states need the first world for markets, investment, capital, and loans. This places the developing world at a constant disadvantage as it puts them in position to better serve the wealthy states more. Dependency and distortion in local developing economies are the result, and national independence is sacrificed for the sake of being globally connected.

Supporters of globalisation argue that free-market capitalism may not always be gentle or kind, but it is the best method to raise the standard of living for the most amount of people. Furthermore, this new international economic system has given many more opportunities to people all over the world. Of course, along with open markets comes an increased mixing and clashing of different cultures and people which can lead to more conflict.

The same theory that shows that free trade is beneficial also shows that globalisation can be harmful to at least one of the trading countries. Moreover, with globalisation, the interests of a country and its companies may diverge causing conflict within. Even domestic disputes can arise over cultural, ethnic, religious, or economic factors as conflict is not limited to international dealings.

Finally, as globalisation brings the world (and its problems) closer together, we also see the rich get richer. Globalisation does not bring about peace or liberation but rather the opposite. It segments populations and furthers the gap between the rich and the poor. By nature, globalised trade is exploitive and conflicting, both within and abroad.

Globalization is the most commonly used word to describe the increasing interconnectedness between nations. In this modern era, it is almost impossible not to be affected by a global issue in some way or another. For example, the strengthening of airport security and scrutiny was felt by all air travellers after the attacks of 9/11. Because of this increased globalization, questions of sovereignty arise much more often than they use to.

Sovereignty is typically defined as supreme independent legal authority. In a contemporary context, this means that every nation has complete control over itself and its domain. Likewise, this means that each nation has no legal control over any other domain. Because there is no overarching legal umbrella to protect external investments or ease conflict, basic international relation theory would suggest that one nation must adhere to the basic tenets of realism: statism, survival, and self-help. Although helping citizens of another country may seem altruistic; it goes against our national sovereignty and independence.

Statism refers to the way realists view the state as the primary actor with unabated power. Because the state is innately sovereign, it is autonomous in its decisions and thus has all the control to make and act on decisions without any overarching authority to regulate or punish the state. This type of system is considered anarchic and was first recognized in 1648 at the Peace of Westphalia and is now referred to as the Westphalian system. The underlying argument here is that because a nation has control within its borders only, that nation should strive to achieve a utilitarian outlook domestically before exporting help. Foreign aid should only be undertaken when domestic threats/problems are alleviated. This is because at the most minimal level, states will seek survival and survival is necessary to attain all other societal goals.

In order to maintain national security and survival, states must use self-help as there is no 'global police' that can be called upon. Although treaties and alliances exist, nothing is etched in stone and there is no higher regulatory power to guarantee anything. This ultimately means that the only state a nation can trust is itself; everything else is subject to the chaotic nature of anarchy. One can not expect foreign help from other countries and must be self-responsible and sustainable in all respects. Helping other countries before your own goes against this tenet and could jeopardize national sovereignty.

To summarize, we noted that statism declares states as principle actors in the Westphalian system with inalienable sovereignty. Once a state is established, the fundamental concern for that state is survival. Once survival is secure, the state can pursue other domestic interests (such as education, health, welfare, etc.). Finally, self-help is the last element which states that nations must help themselves because there is no overarching regulatory force to protect them. The global domain is anarchic and nations within it must solidify their power and security or face the consequences. This comes from the understanding that the state is the main actor and sovereignty is its distinguishing trait. It is hard to argue that we owe more to citizens of another country than our own when looked through a lens of international theory. Nonetheless, it is still possible to help both domestic and foreign people; but the question will always fall back on whether or not the domestic help is adequate enough to warrant foreign aid... and it almost never is.